STONEGROUND

Stoneground

Stephen Allen

THE HOBNOB PRESS

First published in the United Kingdom in 2023

by The Hobnob Press,
8 Lock Warehouse, Severn Road, Gloucester GL1 2GA
www.hobnobpress.co.uk

British Library Cataloguing in Publication Data
A catalogue record for this book is available from the British Library

ISBN 978-1-914407-54-3

Typeset in Adobe Garamond Pro 12/14 pt.
Typesetting and origination by John Chandler

Cover photograph: Sunrise at Hound Tor with Hay Tor in the background. ©Jan-Eric Österlund, reproduced with permission.

Contents

PART 3

PREFACE

The poems in this collection broadly reflect upon the relationship between humans, and other living things, and the rocks, water and air that are so vital for our individual and collective spirit. Most are set in a personal timeframe from childhood to the present, and some are timeless or contemplate the deep past. Much of the imagery draws on a close and visceral perception of the hills, forests, moors and rivers of the West Country, and the fells of Cumbria and the Peak District. Several draw on other places of personal significance, particularly Zambia and Hong Kong. The poems can all be taken at face value, though most have a metaphorical layer or two, or abstractions that are just out of sight of the obvious, for those who like to delve. In each section the poems are ordered with a rough chronology to lend the reader enough structure, though none of the pieces is dependent on that arrangement. The majority were written in 2021-23 and most have not been published previously. Those that have appeared in various journals and magazines are as follows:

The rains return in Zambia, Café Writers, March 2023 (awarded a commendation prize)
Gimmer, Climber Magazine, May 2023
Diamond deep (as Dancing in the rain), Friends of the Lake District, February 2023
Hisley bridge, The Dawntreader, Autumn 2023
Fell running, The Cannon's Mouth, June 2023
Dart nexus, Down Tor circle and row, We came upon a spring, Littoral Magazine, March 2023
Teazel, The Crank, issue 8, 2023
King of the moor, Tap into Poetry, issue 3, 2023
Brink, Tap into Poetry, issue 4, 2023
Superfortress, Village life, Salopeot, Summer 2023
Ted Hughes's stone, Littoral Magazine, June 2023
Living horn, The Crank, issue 9, 2023

PART 1

We came upon a spring

Roaming in St Catherine's Wood
By chance, we came upon a spring
I well recall it, freeze-frame clear
As visions, sounds and smells appear
From deep in the mental scrapbook
Of a distant childhood memory
And the secret we were moved to swear
Below the swaying nests of rooks

For we three boys of the forest floor
All wild springs had a sure mystique
But this one rose in Sulien form
With a flinty taint and slightly warm
That made a subtle bosky bower
With verdant growth in a frosty March
So, favoured by a singing wren
We lingered there upon the hour

We never told another soul
About the faintly thermal font
Of Diana's quiet warm retreat
In ivy-tangled boughs and rocks
Guarded by a vigil-robin
With wary deer and light-foot fox
The place for us was so profound
I hope it has not since been found

Village life

A 1960s Sunday afternoon in Spring
The sound of rooks and the smell of roast
With a damp breeze carrying from the West
The melancholic peace of an eight-bell peal
Filtered by new leaves on a hawthorn hedge
While apple blossom glamour was awaited
Beneath the constant drifting blanket-cloud
That rationed light and questioned aspiration

Earlier that day devotees turned out
In patched up cars and old wool coats
With a fragile acceptance of feudal leftovers
To follow the last hunt of the season
Careful not to startle the horses or hounds
Or speak for any subversive or imaginative reason
While chapel congregations declined, culled by dullness
And The Church sowed the seeds of its diminution

But the rivers and their woods felt true, and still do
Fish and bird domains, remainders of the wild time
Ambassadors of the deep past, ready to act
In the search for timeless purpose
While the small streams flowed to a wider water
Their stately departure a dignified example
For leaving yet staying, renewing yet preserving
An aquatic bellwether that leads to the future

Royal visit

It was a warm still gnat-dance day
And we fished dreamily above the weir
Then two swans skim-landed, like sea planes,
Too big and white for our small river,
And shifted our boyish mise en scene

We fished on regardless, at first,
Then villagers arrived with admonitions
Not to hurt the swans or try to catch one
Because they belong to the Queen
And can break your arm if angered

We sat and fished and felt accused
And longed for our usual coots and ducks
Those avian commoners of the riverbank
That claimed no special-case protection
But were brother-safe enough alongside us

The swans left noisily that afternoon
While we quietly watched our lines
Fresh allegations of dereliction were made
Feeding the swans, not feeding the swans
But the royal visit was soon forgotten

Morning after

A fox's footprints in the hoar
Snuffle-spots where the titbits lay
So, I was second on the scene
The morning after bonfire night
Up at dawn to gather and glean
The frosted fireworks, spent and bright

The roaring fire was adult-time
We children had to stand and watch
Never allowed to light the fuse
That sent the rockets free and high
Nor wonderingly pick and choose
The next one launched into the sky

This pyrotechnic party-time
Was noted for its sausage rolls
Toffee apples and hot pea soups
But I was always keen to see
The glowing remnants fall in groups
And waiting to be found by me

So, in the crackling morning light
With rooks a-chatter to the South
I sought those brilliant cardboard tubes
My foundling many-coloured gems
Their mystique slightly out of mind
Gift of an acrid sulphur smell
Mixed in a wisp of bramble smoke
With a lingering hint of visiting fox
And no one there to say or tell
How to arrange them in my box

Beadle

We breached the seal of the estate
If caught, we could feign being lost
But, of course, we were not
It was a deliberate subversive trespass
To explore, tingled by risk, a forbidden horizon-wood
Moreover, the enterprise was a success
An hour graced by partridges and novelty
Until a red-faced man rode up on a field hunter
Apparently, we were clearly intent on poaching
Notwithstanding our youth and lack of weapons
Our curiosity must have been a provocation
As was our air of innocent disdain
So, he tried to bleed away our feral purpose
And transfuse us with, he said, the social order
Like a beadle on a heckle-horse
Lecturing on the stained-hand guilt of ambition
Be hewers of water, wood and rock, know your station
Bedellus rex, or rather, bedellus absurdum, we thought
A minor gas-planet orbiting the landed star
Such is the tyranny of small power
In the claw-down well-shaft of sulphury stale small places
He watched, seated silent, high and sad, as we left
But we instinctively felt his deferent distress
A prisoner of the cap-doffing world
Trapped face-down in corn in a land of plenty

River's heart

Standing mid-water
Seeing, breathing, listening
Learning the stream-tongue

Easy words at first
Trout rise, vole splash, warbler call
Then feel the unseen

Understanding dawns
Revealed to the journeyman
Know the river's heart

And, uncannily
Sense beneath a rippling rock
A stone loach waiting

Metamorphosis

Past the lonely grey stone farms, we tramped
Looking for the rest of the world, as children will,
Through Cotswold woodlands that we sensed
As being suspended at the beginning of time
Quiet and sad they were in November
Offering no hunting hawk or elusive red squirrel
To affirm the necessity of our journey
Just distant rooks and trees in slumber

A metamorphosis grew from that hike
With the silent sowing of a wander-seed
And its consequential germination
That showed us how to know the need
To see and feel a bigger place to roam
And take the risks and feed the spores
For as boys we yearned for greater lives
Then as men we left for sundry shores

Porth Legh

Porth Legh is pure Kernow
Call it King's Cove if you wish
Then the mystery will mostly evade you
With its geo-natural excise-vexing romance
And hectic history of rum smuggling
A deep clear cauldron with open-sea fish
A pelagic enclave splitting the granite prominence
Lilliputian ocean, shallows and deeps

Wandering in a summer trance
The cove appeared as if by gift
Toting my old cane rod, by chance
(a legacy of tangible encouragement from Uncle Hubert)
I knew I must make contact with this water
Particularly the enchanting steep rift
Where the clear water lost its light to depth
Just beyond the edge of the kelp
So, I cast to the limit of my boyish strength
As the dropping sun picked out the spectral sand
And from that perfect place came Gurnard and John Dory,
Corkwing Wrasse, and some I have forgotten
The dramatis personae of an ancient flowing story
Of water, rocks and living things, from earth and fire
begotten

Riverbank

Art of the casual
The luck of a skimming stone
Thirteen leaps and a disappearance
Carefully chosen, expertly thrown
Recycled by a single use
Natural selection

Passing along
Through clouds of floodlit gnats
Revealed in play by the springtime sun
While serenaded by a mistle-song
High in the knowing sperm-oak
Everything watches

Rustle generator
In the bankside urchin-world
Water voles take up title again
Their reach and range unfurled
Once rarer than a perfect skim-stone
Now, watched by an owl

December

An oak moon falls and dims at dawn
While grasses glint at minus one
The eastern glow flash-gilds the lake
With rose gold mist-shafts, briefly seen
Lighting up a vixen's breath
As lapwings stand to face the sun

Thus, the Cailleach veils the fields
The Queen of Winter has her say
A gift from Fionn's passage tomb
In remembrance of December's gloom
She visits later than yesteryear
Though now the frost defines the day

So, a morning made for ice and crows
Now sings loudly in still bright air
As cautious creatures warm and wend
To old promises of food and friends
And take the rhythmic cold in hand
Rejecting the lapse-tune of despair

Next corner

Footpath drifters find new worlds
Just around their next corners
Blended into place by a warm damp rain
With swaying boughs in a wandering wind
Or baked-in with the buzzing crickets of July
Below the vigilant lark-trill at midday
Water washed, sun dried, the elemental cycle
Then mesmerized by a rocky stream
The sounds, the smells, the creatures
Buzzard cry, finch gossip
The ultimate awareness of Wren
And a sunset heron's still silhouette
Beside a brook-pool
Where small fish rise to feed
And learn both the poles of predation
The drifter briefly imagines all such places
And understands it is vital
To remain part of what has been seen
By walking toward a bend in the path

Shelter

The setting-out had started well
With dry-foot warmth and a following breeze
To cross the moor in a single day
He vowed to take it on with ease
And all alone, just himself to please

But gathering in the pallid sky
Beyond the lens of fair-day cloud
The eastern sky grew tall and dark
Ready to cast its chilling shroud
Upon such hubris unavowed

It caused an unexpected shock
When sudden pouncing wind and rain
Struck his complacent hike with force
So, with likely triumph on the wane
His intended goal was all in vain

From a need for shelter to survive
He cast about for a bothy or cave
And was gifted with a crag-foot crack
That drew him with its open-clave
To a small dry room, his life to save

And there he sat and thawed and thought
His first still day for many years
Then saw the drawings on the walls
Of deer and people, fires and spears
An ancient peoples' joys and fears

He felt a newfound lightness there
Where refuge left a human trace
And a distant kinship with the folk

Who needed safety in the place
That warmed his blood and saved his face

Upon return he reflected well
How true hearts have a fragile flame
To embrace brave humility
And eschew vanity courts no blame
As boastful words can lead to shame

Since that deep instructive day
The memory was his balm for strife
A meditative remedy
When threatened by the jealous knife
On the blasted heaths of ambitious life

Seeing others

I once knew a man
An instinctive denier
With a judging mind
Encrusted with a limescale
Of preconception
Unable to navigate
The stormy waters
Of the particular lives
Of unknown others.
Empathy and perception
Were lost bright metals
Beneath his chalk-stiff thinking
Dried by the long fume
And simmering resentment
Of his kettle-brain.

One day he confessed
To having had a nightmare
During a fever
In which a vivid vision
Laid a golden path
That passed beyond firm reason
To a floodlit place
Where people changed their senses
And swapped their spirits
Blending their flaws and faults
Forgiving offenses
Finding kindness and respect.

But relief was near
He woke fresh the next morning
And all was normal

Makeshift incense

Thin lavender smoke
Sultry still garden-fire haze
Deep memory switch

Bramble was added
Vivid change in the mind-scene
Grandfather's garden

Clod-grass and tussock
Smouldering against drystone
Perfumed the orchard

Fallen apple smell
Mixed with the makeshift incense
Can raise a new smile

Endeavour

Ill-defined rumours were started
Of snakes under stones near Rock Pond
Thus was our future determined
For two days at least in July
Three of us braved the thick jungle
Those exotic creatures to find
Sustained by an unripe apple
And cheese sandwich gone rather dry
By late afternoon we were tired
Nettle-stung, thorn-scratched and hot
Ready to blame all and sundry
Who spoke the reptilian lie
Then next day we started afresh
Sleep let the endeavour take root
The snakes were quickly discovered
The tall tale we could verify
Oddly, we kept it a secret
How we rudely entered their place
Ashamed of our childish hubris
In sending wild spirits awry.

Source

Roaming, we found
Damp and soupy pots of fog
Collecting above an autumn borne
Fugitive water brief and bright
Below the web-strewn St John's wort
Fated to drain away and join
A brooklet in a promised state

Parallel, we followed
Over the passive wetted stones
Rapid-teased and liver-smooth
Coalescing stream by stream
To make the languid flowing form
That has a heart-place in a dream
Of peace and stillness, wren-song pure

Seated, we watched
Where drifting dandelion seeds
Symbolized our wandering thoughts
Unfocussed in the midday light
We felt the river's growing strength
And surety between the reeds
Reflective of the power to leave

Inspired, we continued
Great ponds and races then appeared
Where, dammed and channelled for the mills
The flow was once a slave to work
Now these are graced by dragonflies
And lie between the chalky hills
Their time in industry fulfilled

Eventually, we knew

Our river abruptly sacrificed
Its character to bigger worlds
Joining the Avon in fine spate
Engulfed and lost but nonetheless
In grand and seemly time, we saw it
Leaving, mixing, growing stronger

Roam-and-seek

Drifting lakeside along the gradient of time
We looked for a perfect skimming stone
Rarer than a copper dragonfly
Glinting in the shatter-light
Among discarded swan-mussel shells
That never gave a single pearl
What might put the mundane past to flight?

A trodden quest for specialness
Touchstones of the singular
Like those cross-grain renegades of Nature
Of which we never seemed to tire
On our restless roam-and-seek
And to glimpse a peregrine or otter
Provided a simple glow of purpose

Change of state

We felt a drive to wander far
A restless need to find and claim
The eerie woods and crystal streams
Both novel yet familiar
It was a joy to find a brook
That none of us had seen before
To hear its song and take a look
An impulse we could not ignore

Then sirened by a grey-noise roar
We found the water's change of state
From stately flow above the weir
To river running fast and shallow
Glinted by its surface chaos
Split by sun and oaken shadow
Hustling past the common bugloss
It played its tune on rounded rocks

Soon, the scene became familiar
Its unique magic-heart subsumed
And fishing upstream from the dam
Seemed like any other water
But with pride in our discovery
We spun our gaudy spoons for perch
As winter blew in cold and blustery
Then, affirming our title with delight
We saw a dipper dive the rapids
And herons stalking in the reeds

Too tidy for snakes

Village of the year
Proclaims the sign beside the road
Then, we see the over-petted lawns
And hostile netted bird-proof thatch
Perched upon the limestone deceptions
Of Cotswold hovels-cum-mansions
Where stiffening parish rules demand
A danegeld on acceptability
Tested by confession in the Ancient Inn
Through leafy Laurie Lee idylls
Tuned to a rose-tinted tomorrow
With just a touch of forbidding
And troubled glances at the long barrow
With its quiet accusative memory
Of all the natural wildness lost
In a world now too tidy for snakes

Teazel

Near where the downland flint-pile lies
A pair of chalky rounded stones,
Split by a teazel's restless rise,
Gave pass to an upstart green-spring stalk
That set apart their limestone bones

Reaching soon a flower-burst length
The bloom pushed out its petal-head
Projecting forth with urgent strength
The scented code of generation
Imperative for pollen-spread

And once the bees had done their deed
The head swayed to a gentle beat
Casting away the new-formed seed
Then, fading through a fugitive pink,
Retreated with its work complete

The river at Cerne Abbas

The Cerne is oozing newly free
From its birth-spring, high and wild
The latent gift of ancient rocks
With water purified by age
Not yet abstracted or defiled

While trendle-dancers on the hill
Sing for the far-off Nine Stones ring
To celebrate from Earth and sky
The stream born from the limey loins
Unseen below the tumuli

It quickly gathers rippled light
A haven for the native trout
And sleekit grayling, small and quick
That reassert their timeless right
From deep instinctive memory

Shunning the Giant's glaring pride
The river passes with disdain
His chalky club and missing hide
That seem to say all must admire
His priapic decoration

Then, blending with the courtly Frome
The Cerne concludes with quiet flow
Its pristine prehistoric task
Of draining rain from times untold
To shimmer seaward, clean and cold

Summer fishing

Heat imperative
Wary creatures out of sight
Quarry-chasm deep

End of the stillness
Warm rain on the shaded lake
Reflexion misted

The change is sensed
Viscous movements can be seen
Heaving the topskin

Conditions are right
Apex-fish have been waiting
Water politics

Perfect dry-fly cast
First presentation that day
Predator rises

PART 2

King of the moor

Wren stands on a weathered tor
Small, quick and unafraid
A worry for the knowing Celts
Flitting from the wran-boy raid
To revel in its pert contempt
For lesser birds and roaring men

With a burst of unmatched sound
The bird-king sings the laws
Heard by every rook and jay
And all with wings and claws
So, woe betide the feathered nests
Of subjects with subversive thoughts

The eagle and the condor bow
Before this tiny archosaur
Trapped inside a custom-well
Re-proclaimed across the moor
Its given right to rule the air
They never think to challenge

It is a trick of confidence
That keeps the Wren in power
Seen, then not seen, within a trice
Then proclaiming from a tower
In a voice that can't be questioned
Emitted from a legend-throne

Wistman's Wood

Lacy Dartmoor dawn
Spider webs refract the sun
Wistman's Wood lights up

Down in the clatter
As wrens tick their snake alarm
The day starts alert

Message from deep time
This is how the moor-woods were
Moss and lichen draped

They will be renewed
Spreading from contorted oaks
Seeding sanity

Charm our sylvan selves
With the resilient boughs
Dartmoor influence

Black-a-Tor copse

Along the Okement river trail
We hiked in darkness from below
To pay respect and stand before
The pristine copse at Black-a-Tor

With first light leaking from the east
The footpath seemed less haunted, so
Tinners' huts could shed their wraiths
And tunnel back to reason-time

Green and firm, the rain-doused heaths
Saw dewy grasses hiss and glow
While Venus risen bright and blue
Made tawny owl a mortal bird

He shed his spirit-air at dawn
And left the dark and wizened wood
Where cryptic nightingales once flew
Though now their songs are seldom heard

But in the fresh and reborn day
The ancient oaks and mossy stones
Predicted futures for the moor
Of living forest tor-to-tor

Then, after the Anthropocene
A parliament of birds will meet
And by decree it will restore
All lost avian melodies

Tawhead at dawn

Yes Tor looming grey
Ego hides in raven-form
Deceptive plumage

Below Hangingstone
By the small awakened Taw
A memorial

Knowing stars recede
Wet sheen gilds the poet's stone
Reclining remote

Brooding, barely known
Rook and fox of modern verse
Supplicate for spawn

Anointed by rain
Source of coalescing streams
A river is made

Stony-bedded brooks
With water-sirens calling
Sacred salmonids

Fog-shine grows brighter
Throws a glitter in the dew
Mystery sustained

Ted Hughes's stone

A curiosity of words
Drew us off the high firm path
On spongy turf to Taw Head Seep
That drizzle-days had rendered soft
To find the subtle poet-stone
That lichens gild and ravens keep
Above the brook, it lies alone

The water garners as it drops
Until a nascent river runs
To where the poet stood and looked
Under those hazy Dartmoor suns
Into the trout and grayling stream
Intensely happy, crow-nail free
In a revenant salmon-dream

The unobtrusive granite slab
Lies tussock-low and settled firm
Beneath the rise of Hangingstone
Its fitting nature meets the man
Who knew this harsh but calming place
And understood its blood and bone
Yet saw its light and felt its grace

Living horn

We traipsed in single silent file
To where the sessile oaks crawl up
From ancient acorns lost in moss
When mystery defined the moors

And there we saw beside the copse
A straightened tree of modern cast
That rose up to the westward sun
With clenching roots and handsome shaft

It seemed its trunk was breaking free
Eschewing life in stunted form
Standing on a boulder-pair
From which it drew exquisite fare

And so, we felt the message clear
In silence, to admire the wood
Was supplication well enough
To all the free and fertile world

So, while an unperceptive friend
Bored us with an ivy-myth
We moved up to that living horn
And stroked the bark that sucked the stones

Hisley bridge

Shade-lit at midday
Hisley bridge of roughcut stone
Arches the shingle bank

Moss and ivy coat
Bedraggles the reflection
Lowering the light

Dartmoor irony
A structure made by humans
Denotes wilderness

Stone craft repurposed
Once was a horse and hay route
Now photo-fodder

Avian retreat
A sunlit flash of yellow
Wagtail returning

Looking down

Tramping south from Cosdon Hill
The view to the east ten miles at least
To lower scapes of fields and farms
Where serried swathes of linn and wheat
Seem out of kilter with the moor
Then, with such philosophic thoughts
On buzzing fells in rising heat
The fugue of walking comes with ease
Surrounded by forsaken land
Where nimble spirit-echoes roam
Like birdsong on the morning breeze
From ancient temples near at hand
With time, a human logic speaks
Of soul space on the rugged tors
And wholesome crops on the fertile soil
Their vital stewardship restored

Dart nexus

The East Dart flows ceaselessly
Through a mystery of mossy woods
And spate-cut clefts through granite scour
With downstream runs that drop and roar
Into the clear deep amber pools
That pause its hurry to the sea

Glimpsed from slightly out of sight
The stream draws creatures from their paths
To sense its spirit, primal-pure
Unsullied in the Anthropocene
Among the fleeting insect lives
And ancient pristine river-stones

A pilgrim to that nexus came
Called by thin forsaken bonds
A hominid at the water's edge
She felt a presence in the deep
And wondered if her dreams were true
Then lighted by a silver flash
The depths confirmed the neo-myth
That fully savage salmonids
Still grace the Dart with fertile spawn
Compelled, like many wanderers
To mark their prehistoric dawn
And so, they met across a glance
An instant accidental truce
Two unacquainted predators
Astonished by each other's eyes

Buzzard looks and listens

As thin east light marks the way
Small flowers awake
Fine moor scents start gathering
Clouds forsake the day

To the northeast a stone row sits
Temple to the natural world
A resilient remnant, barely worn
A compass for the rising sun
Unsullied by the old iron pits
And those who dug for tin and gold
Now a granite Dartmoor throne
Where mistle thrushes sing laments
For saurian stories rarely told
Of eagle-kings and crafty wrens

Then,
Buzzard flies up gracefully
And, buzzard rides upon the breeze
Now the ultimate daylight creature
He watches all that lies below
Looks for carrion, looks for victims
Looks with contempt at the rooks asunder
And all with lowly earthbound lives
Sees so sharp with amber eyes
Calls out high, but not to us
While listening to the mistle's tale

Down Tor circle and row

The dawn lights up the polychrome
On lichen-painted standing stones
That shine where placed by lithic souls
Who must have come from near and far
To feel and see the rhythmic truth
Of sunrise and the morning star

Today a wren sings from upon
The pillar-stone that dominates
And with its small commanding voice
Reminds me of its bird-mystique
Its ancient role as king-of-fowls
Unafraid of the eagle's shriek

Then, to the south a curlew calls
A living echo from the past
Fleeing from a saurian fate
Its sound reflected by the stones
And softened in the drifting mist
In blended other-worldly tones

Wild free creatures live here now
And hold this geometric place
We share their rightful stewardship
And guard its pointer to our past
So, we must sing and supplicate
To make this vital concord last

Spawning

An ancient migrant
On a mortal pilgrimage
Desperate traction

Below the rapids
Sensing one last barrier
Singular purpose

Anticipation
Holding against the current
Depth fortuitous

Mystery trigger
A successful leap is made
Bold and incautious

In the upper stream
After many years at sea
The hen must be blessed

Minotaur

We walked so quietly that day
From Steeperton to Sittaford
Picking through spongy Teignhead tufts
A morning hike of haze and thought
To follow the softer southbound way

But we drifted to a bovid storm
Of rounding up and herd control
By a fierce and ring-fit longhorn bull
A rippling mass of black-eyed musth
Insisting that the cows conform

He saw our careless silhouette
Against the glowing westward sky
Then warned us with an angry snort
Scanning the hillside, scent and sight
Absurdly, saw us as a threat

He stamped and scraped, began to pace
In our direction, beeline-straight
Across the intervening moor
And appeared, head-on, a minotaur
His fury mixed with savage grace

We ran and hid behind a mound
And vanished from his frantic world
His call-sign changed to mark the loss
And with some urgent casting round
He smelled the air and gored the ground

The harem now ignored his bellow
So, he left to bring them into line
And we rose up from our saving-stones

The coombe now feeling harsh and raw
Our reverie no longer mellow

Since that primitive encounter
The spirit of the moor came clear
Not just a park of pleasant paths
But a wormhole made for knowing fear
And a reminder of our frailty

Down Tor ring

A searcher for mysterious wraiths
Heard echoes in old Down Tor ring
Quieter than the ragged rooks
That flew up with indignant cries
And subtler than a piercing wren
That claimed the temple-space to sing

Then, circled by the megaliths
With eyes drawn to a distant hill
The searcher felt wights close at hand
As the ruined beauty of the cairn
Began to press its influence
On sounds arising from the land

The message from a distant time
Spoke not of guilt and sacrifice,
Or virtue in a pain-hard heart,
But true and elemental joy
In life beneath the summer sun
Embracing all of Nature's art

Drizzlecombe

Dartmoor standing stones
Exquisite and abundant
Beyond legal claim

Drizzlecombe menhirs
Endure their lone erosion
Lithic history

Granite witnesses
To all the freedoms stolen
And favours returned

Lost in rock clatter
Their presence seems forbidden
Like bivouac tents

No lasting setback
On a scale of dolmen-time
The mists will rise up

Wild camp

The moor engulfs us
Rising sun has graced our day
Urgency recedes

Hear a curlew call
Mellow in the afternoon
Peace comes with walking

Clamped in a fine mist
Shadows cross a clapper bridge
New memory starts

Sun and moon emerge
To sail above the springhead
Sleeping-place revealed

Agreement is reached
An armistice of purposes
We travelled enough

Pilgrims now seek rest
Hungry for a thrush's song
Among the ant hills

Hay Tor

In the early whiffling moorland breeze
The granite stone-crop's murmurings
Are the epicentre of a choir
Of creatures that make a harmony

Outlines in the bracken hillside
Are footings of a human story
A long but passing farming phase
Metamorphic for the settled fauna

The moor is in recovery
With unknown future incarnations
Its igneous bed seems permanent
With constant change in its living skin

Though today,
On Hay Tor in an April squall
With the mysterious purpose of its force
The West Wind wakes the resting rocks
To silence the Curlew with their song

Stoneground

Haze-hot Dartmoor days
Trickle-streams run quietly
Birds build instinct-nests

A water-lean time
Sharpened selection pressure
Fit creatures prevail

Second broods fledging
Offspring of the stoneground world
Soon ready for flight

Yellow wagtails leave
And dippers turn a pebble
Running rain arrives

Diamond deep

A summer of relentless dry
And smoky dust hangs in the air
The dale head stream has lost its force
So Sour Milk rocks are showing bare

But all can change within a day
And doom-say gives way to rejoice
For Thor's gift rumbles once again
And the wettest valley hears the voice

Soon the gill is newly running
The trickles swell to waterfalls
Each breath smells of clear renewal
The dipper bobs and the stonechat calls

Hikers sluiced down from the mountain
Have caught the spirit of the day
Their chat an impromptu thanksgiving
With a light-foot tread along the way

They descend on tired and tangling legs
Passing the Derwent's diamond deep
Sensing an uneasy renaissance
That might not let the fell tops sleep

The future of this unique place
Requires many selfless acts of faith
Because, the guardians of this terrain
Must be, the children dancing in the rain

Late on Rigghead

Hiking trance
Slowly bleeding light
On the ridge

Raven call
Ruffling the daydream
Slate echo

Earth music
Beck water hissing
Lulled again

Hill rhythm
Mends the reverie
Sun descends

We return
To parallel time
In the dale

Wool Packs

On many a hike
We sheltered at the Wool Packs
High above Edale

Sometimes for the shade
More often from wind and rain
Always for the peace

Shoulder to shoulder
Quiet times of tea and cake
With curlews calling

Small pilgrimages
To the best of our places
True companions

I smell the gritstone
When we speak about those times
Sitting knee to knee

Gimmer

On a chilly brittle Langdale day
With misty sun on Gimmer Crag
We felt a hopeful hubris rising,
Despite a black-eyed raven's warning,
And climbed in a tiptoe crafty style
Through the centre of the cliff
To top a perfect windless morning

We perched among the clifftop stones
Thoughts adrift in the hazy shade
Stilled by a distant curlew piping
A soundtrack for moorland meditation
As silently we each remade
The moves of that ascending line

We would not forget that special time
When light and cloud, and rock and sound
Aligned with music from the wild
And subtle scent-notes from the ground
To form a lasting evocation
Though neither of us voiced it

A sandwich and a flask of tea
Was all the celebration needed
No call for champagne or cigar
Just resting in the limpid light
Our chatter quiet and unheeded
Before the hike back to the car

Though more than forty years ago
The sensory pleasures of that climb,
Its songs and smells and granite touch,
Tumble to mind to reassure

The precedence of place and people
Over tales of fear and derring-do
In mountain memories that endure

Wen Zawn

A spring-sun was struggling, as we were,
To reach the weather side of Mynydd Twr
Then, we came down upon Wen Zawn, drizzle wet
Staring into a cauldron of gulls and spray
And the special light of the Irish sea
Prophesying a storm is on the way
In a rising swell with fractured clouds
So, not a day for climbing, but for seated obeisance
As by all senses we were captured
In the net of a natural glamour
And blessed with a transient gift of looking
Through which we saw, a living-dancing place
Of terns and choughs and diving seals
And the perfect creatures of the cliffs

Burning stone

Deep Cumbrian dark
A briefly disturbing sky
Burning stone landed

Perseus at the door
The end of a long journey
The peat was steaming

Conceived in star-fire
And by the laws of physics
Permitted to land

We paid a visit
Welcome to Andromeda
Who made us feel young

Fell running

The ground lifts light to Edale End
With time to set the running-trance
And find a stride and settled beat
Tuning out the troubled sounds
That vibrate in from mind and sky

Then, rounding through the packhorse bridge
To start the steep and misty climb
On Jacob's Ladder to Kinder Low
Where all is firmly out of mind
Barring footwork, breath and breeze

Over the gritty Downfall path
Deserted in the rising sun
The runner at the highest point
Begins to hear the world again
Water splash and Raven's croak

Past the flowing deep ravine
The sunny level ground begins
A stretch of feeling high and well
That lets the curlew's call be heard
A sprite of joy at last permitted

A few more miles of rhythmic running
Has the demons in retreat
A smile is lit by flitting whinchats
And wheatears spark forgiving thoughts
In a spirit coming up for air

The long a steady downhill canter
Leads back to the darkened dale
Where an alert and serene tiredness

Uplifts the runner's shadow-life
Until repeating-time is near

Water-laden

A furnace sun is rare 'long hereabout
With Langstrath swards becoming crackle-dry
Then one stroke from Taranis ends the drought
And water-laden clouds soon fill the sky
Shortly the sphagnum gives a spongy sigh
When parched runnels slowly start to drain
And mainstreams welcome back the falling rain

We rush to where two steep brooks blend and turn
To celebrate the rebirth of the burn

The ghyll is in a foamy flowing state
It runs between two spray-wet boulder stones
At last, we hear it rumble in full spate
And feel the rock vibrating in our bones
It seems to speak with icy undertones
With subtle coded questions as to why
The dale head had become so very dry

The query was of course from deep inside
The conscience-stones we carry with false pride

Perspective

A balmy dreamworld on the moor
A chance to wander on the fell
The last of this year's shirtsleeve hikes
Autumn's Indian summer spell
With bold plans to eschew the camp
And sleep al fresco like a tramp

But as shadows reach toward the east
A restless churn beneath the sun
Signals a fundamental change
And intentions need to be undone
No staring at the stars tonight
The shelter must be weathertight

An urgency comes into play
To find sound ground to pitch the tent
Among a boulder's leeside ferns
Damage by broadside to prevent
The newfound purpose very plain
A refuge from the coming rain

The broad brush of a northwest wind
Starts to wet-wash tor and vale
Then as the dusk light falls and fades
Night is gripped by the rising gale
So, birds and bats forego the air
Leaving the skyline cold and bare

The storm blows cold and wet for hours
And thunder punctuates the roar
But in the tent, it's warm and dry
The soup a treat like none before
So, it seems, on calm reflexion

When in a cold and hostile place
A little tarp becomes a mansion

Arena

A dragonfly hunts
In the stilling evening light
Above a small stream

It shows clear purpose
Quartering the horsetail reeds
Seizing dancing gnats

From our rocky perch
We watch with fascination
Predator and prey

We cheer with bright eyes
The insect gladiator
Dartmoor arena

We can feel the chase
Deeply alive within us
Pulling at our roots

Superfortress

Winter Bleaklow dawn
Foggy loom of stone and peat
An eye corner glimpse
Reveals a sharp disturbance
Metal artefacts
The Superfortress midden
Post war pterosaur
Stripped of its integument
Engine monuments
Reduced by time and water
Permitted litter
Below rocks on Higher Shelf
The fatal furrow
Just moss and forgetfulness
One among many

The stone cutter Daniel Gumb

Was that a robin in Gumb's Cave?
Bodmin's bothy near the Keuswask
A fleeting glance and no fine song
Fitting for that shallow hovel
So, I won't swear it, if you ask

It might have been his fleghes wraiths
Swirling on the brink of seeing
Chanting how they did no wrong
To pay no dues to England's king
For Daniel's geometric task

But then it flew in sight again
And trilled a message plainly heard
It was no robin but a wren
The most subversive of all birds
Skipping through that stony den

It sang of Kernow's ancient pride
Then praised afresh the mason's stance
The nation's growing self-belief
That Kernowyon might foresee
Their future in the sky's expanse

In a Magwitch state

He slipped the work-gang in the dark
And fled into the fresh free moor
An act that was the incarnation of the dream
He fabricated on the borders of his sanity
As he lay in his stone-cold cell
Of disappearing, never to be seen again
So, he ran through the cool and cleansing rain

After ten miles of howling damp
He slumped to the lee side of a tor
With rising anger at his Magwitch state
Where were the signs of a new beginning?
He felt betrayed by his own imagination
Then his hold on wakefulness began to slacken
And he drifted into sleep among the bracken

He dreamt of,
Stumbling through the wasteland of his conscience
With fugitive fragments of remorse
Teasing his peripheral vision but denying focus
But they could not be admitted, of course
And were destined to remain rejected orphans
Of the scorched hinterland of his reason
That saw all resistance as a personal treason

There was no magic wormhole of escape
As dogs and police came with the dawn
To return him to his wondering-cell
Just another lifer settling in
With his grip on reality on the rocks
Wishing he could run beyond the moorland murk
But lacking the wherewithal to make it work

Grand soft day

The morning walk was overdue
And sunny drizzle called us out
Casting mystery on the view
With distant woodlands barely seen

A grand soft day, the Irish say
Perfectly light and warm and wet
Southerly weather has a way
Of giving life a sanguine sheen

Then, in the subtle light of lent
A draggled creature crossed our path
With body thin and spirit spent
What was this vision, sad and mean?

A homeless vixen on the run
Fleeing her ancestral den
Evicted by a Scarlet's gun
When blackthorn trees turn nascent green

And so, the vulpine refugee
Hurried by with a scornful glance
Perceiving that for you and me
The day would soon be soft again

Alpha vixen

Red fox finds her way
Cold and droopy winter fog
Levitating gait

Dawn adds a sparkle
Flanking-bright the vixen's trail
Single-minded trot

Carrying night prey
Culmination of her work
A self-worthy proof

Then day breaks mist-green
Pointing up the pheasant's cape
Red, white, blue and rust

In her rock-roof den
She consumes the sacrifice
Feeding a mystique

Dream and wait

He knows he must retain the land
This red-haired remnant of the ice
With iron purpose to prevail
Enduring any sacrifice

The wolf and bear have long since gone
So, all things must be his to take
To move and strike as he sees fit
A vulpine world now free to make

But now he feels a deep-set fear
His domination will not wax
As humans with their dogs and guns
Will wield the power that he lacks

So, from a foray he returns
A stoic home-grown refugee
To hide within the stony land
His den below the old yew tree

A mellow glow shows in the East
With Reynard slipping through the mist
A hint of hurry in his gait
To go to ground, to dream and wait

Artillery

In a silent copse
Sensing a deep infra-sound
A vixen listens

Something is perturbed
Precision not forthcoming
The vixen listens

Neither horse and hounds
Nor spaniel, man and gun
Form such a cadence

No alarm sounding
Wren and robin not ticking
Nothing approaches

Within the fox-realm
Artillery bombardment
Inconsequential

Privilege

The walk across to Heron Quays
Was blustered by a midnight squall
That gave the faint snow lift and spin
And made the dead leaves rise and fall

Then through the angle of an eye
A hot and living shadow ran
Into the lime of diode white
To cross the plaza's widest span

Now a fox was clearly seen
When glittered by the Christmas lights
Its confidence was on display
A doyen of the urban nights

It caught a scenting from the east
And veered off to investigate
The bounty of a back door bin
Fussily picking what it ate

The fox has tapped its privilege
And learned to play the greedy game
Down among the glossy docks
Where dogs are few and rather tame

Why live among the rural rooks
And run the risk of hounds and gun
When here beside the steel and glass
The main concern is number one

So, the canyons of Canary Wharf
Are where the fox will make a life
Among the people who admire
The way it thrives on guile and strife

The countryman

He thought of himself as a countryman
Outdoors, spotting, naming, claiming
Always collecting,
Owning things to save them
The sort of contradictory soul
Who loves birds and steals their eggs
Guarding any justification with
Granite edging at the rim of a conscience
Too hearty by half
Endless commentary but no insight
Noisily announcing a presence
That ploughed an exodus before him
Bashing verge-flowers with a restless stick
Issuing orders to his barging dog
Hearing no beauty in a blackbird's song
Nor seeing the eternity in a wren's sharp eye
But in his solitary home
He often had the faint sense of a void
Centred on a candle-flicker of self-knowledge
And sought an explanation in the unreflective gaze
Of his stuffed barn owl

The guide

It was all just corny theatre
And uncaringly cynical too
A glaringly obvious act
Ignoring the doubtful wry looks
Repeating each dubious fact
Just bluffing through the nature tours
With breezy borrowed metaphors,
And a knack for disconnection
Hiding behind the squandered smiles

Later, slack-faced and unscripted
He crossed a live meadow to find,
A space he thought of as empty
But came face to face with a hind
Their eyes stayed welded together
Until she felt ready to leave
Then turning she fled from the scene
While he stood light and uncertain
Bereft of the ice in his spleen

Dreoilín

A hiker's reverie was split
One morning in the early frost
When summoned from his dreamy amble
By a haunting urgent melody
Bursting from the tangled bramble
That lay beside the stony track

The singer was the King of Birds
The nimble crafty Dreoilín
A wren in mystic incarnation
Ruling-sprite of the misty dawn
Whose close-up call went to the core
To light a blend of glee and caution

The sooth-bird spelled an alteration
In the mood-ghost of the day
So, intrigued by the forthright song
The hiker brightly knew a duty
To think upon the cryptic message
And feel the triller's arcane knowledge

Chesil

Pelagic fish of the open sea
Are pulled by bait-lights set at night
To a shore of graded tumble-stones
That rattle in the hissing foam
So boatless fishers' lines can reach
Their quarry close to Chesil Beach

This currency of leisure time
Was once a hunt for vital food
The tombolo a unique form
Of trespass in the deeper swell
Allowing proximity of cast
To ease the famines of the past

Lerret-boats had floundered there
Despite the oarsmen's strength and skill
And souls were lost to the undertow
Coming to rest in a pebbly grave
But, shoals of fish can ease the plight
Of hungry urchins in their flight

Midden

A perceptive walker met the coast
Where melt-moraines abut the sea
Unknowingly to stand atop
Of midden mounds of flint and shell
And felt there an affinity
That reached into a time and place
When objects dropped would leave a trace
Of Mesolith prosperity

Too easily we might assume
That stone-age life was torn with fear
But midden-throwers occupied
These precious points for centuries
Replete with food and stone so near
Perfecting spears to hunt the boar
Fireside tales to spin the lore
Of human continuity

Eventually, the wood and flint
Gave way to copper, zinc and tin
That made the story-changing bronze
Then huts and pots and politics
Thus, modern metal-times began
So, the midden-mix of knap and bone
Became a forgotten reliquary
An antique echo of the past
And, foreteller of our destiny

PART 3

Pebble music

Granite mother-stone
Endured an earth-shatter day
Laying pebble spawn

Wave-washed back and forth
Millions of collisions
Old pebble music

No shape repeated
An entropic orchestra
Pebble factory

The singing has paused
A hundred chosen pebbles
Rest in my newt pond

Driving rain

A storm was brewing, we were told
The warm-and-wet was near its peak
When straight-down windless torrents fall
To drench the vast miombo woods
Of Zambia and Mozambique
So, heavy rain was coming soon
But we must take the empty road

Hours of driving through the night
Below the restless thunder-clouds
As forests shed their blackest light
When briefly touched by headlamp beams
All ragged roadside bundu grass
And over-arching dripping trees
With steamy rain and millipedes

The engine's pulse and wiper's splash
The track's hypnotic tinnitus
Often broken by a flash
Of brain-resetting super-white
That showed the treescape vividly
And emphasized our lonely path
Between the swamps and wooded hills

We swept past silent village huts
Their oil lamps doused and doorways dark
Just lingering fragrant woody smoke
The trace of people, resting warm
While sleepy guard dogs rose to bark
At our tail-lights cruising through
As midnight reformed in our wake

Through the wild and pristine land

We glided in our car-cocoon
Glimpsing through the windscreen glass
Serval cats and a baboon clan
In a rarely-pondered wilderness
Just beyond our faint reflections
The stark domain of Darwin's rules

When through a slow and greyscale dawn
We climbed the hill that holds our town
With cockerel calls and stands of corn
We knew then we were safely home
So, children on the backseat woke
Then leapt up freshly unrestrained
And started looking for their friends

Walking to the well

The eastern pack of morning stars
Becomes less diamond-bright
And the crickets quieten on cue
As the first pink pushes up the blue
And a small girl becomes a water wraith
Walking to the well, a solo spirit
This is her daily unwatched time
Free to softly dream at dawn
Her solitaire of new ideas
About why the can falls deeper
And the rope seems longer
Than in her mother's well-days
Or why the snakes are fewer
And there are no leopards
To keep the watchdogs wary
Then, the sun is up to dry the air
And make the village shadow-fine
The bell for school has now proclaimed
That the girl must go to learn by line
Another version of her future

The rains return in Zambia

Across the vast miombo woods
We fix a stare and supplicate
To the electric heart that beats
In thunder-drums from westerly
As massing, flickering lantern clouds
Grow laden with the rain we crave

Teasing light-shows draw in closer
While children, cats and dogs lie languid
On our hopeful evening-stoep
In treacly end-of-dry-time air
Every creature deeply longing
For water's atavistic care

In time,
A flash of image-freezing force
Brings a straight-down perfect teem
That transforms the spirit of the day
And presents the pure transcendent gift
Of running rain that allows all life
And for me,
To feel renewed and see again
My children dancing in the rain

Sous verre

Barriers rise in many forms
Like invisible walls of glass
Allowing through their rigid films
The teasing photons cleared to pass

But lasting insights can arise
When open souls abut the fence
To gaze with fresh and youthful eyes
Enlightened by their innocence

And so, two children came to find
A shield-bug stranded in a jar
And wondered if it might be kind
To name it for a shooting star

They showed it to a Bemba friend
"Qu'est-ce c'est tu as sous verre"?
(He liked to use his Congo French)
"We call a star Ntanda here"

The youngsters had no language airs
So hoovered up the vivid words
And shield-bugs thus became "soovares"
Both then and ever afterwards

The shield-bug brilliantly green
Took to the wing and flew away
To be the metaphoric sheen
Upon that boundary-breaking day

Mwela rock paintings

Faded antelopes
Red renditions by the Twa
Flee in frozen time

Hunters depicted
Generic shape and colour
Close to the abstract

Some vanishing-faint
Fugitives from the cave walls
Emancipation

Others vibrant-bright
Messengers of their makers
This is how it was

Chalk and slate

A woman from Lusaka
Stood by Bangweulu
"Where the water meets the sky"
And islands of papyrus
Shimmer with birdsong
A choir to the quiet Twa
Her grandmother's people
For whom no one spoke of loss
Of words and knowledge
Or of worth and traditions
In that shrinking-time
As subsuming continued

She started to feel a new guilt
Descendent remorse
"When the present meets the past"
For her lack of principle
To see, to hear, to speak
Of the loss of tongue and stories
Expressed in earth-red
On the rocks of the plateau
But there was no stone
In the swamp of last retreat
Nothing scratched or drawn
Remembrance was cut and lost

Inspired by the bird-spirits
She resolved to act
"As a conscience meets a fate"
Penning a freshly cogent case
To pierce the heated din
And surfeit of certainty
Of the law-talkers

A metaphoric painted rock
Calling for redress
Ancestral equality
A new chalk and slate

Los Roques

We wade the shallow vast lagoon
The water warm within the reef
Seeking shoals of ghostly fish
That cast a shadow on the sand
And in the middle-distance now
A mangrove patch, the only land
All else, the domes of sky and sea
Enclose a perfect sense of space

Pelicans glide the low wet air
Sentinels of this pristine world
Echoing a long Jurassic reign
With ancient saurian silhouettes
This is a fish and fowl domain
A refuge on a coral base
Where many tired migrating birds
Rest in this rich and shielded place

Under the humming morning sun
We walk and look, walk and look
Glued to an atavistic fate
To find the fish and cast a fly
Then when we hook and celebrate
And meet our wild catch eye-to-eye
We treat him with ancestral care
Until he leaves for the Carib Sea

Consensus

Many paths converge
Leading down to Big Wave Bay
Where purposes meet

Fish, birds and surfers
Putting on their gladdest rags
For the mating dance

The sea is watching
Timeless but impermanent
As its dragon-waves

Fish, birds and surfers
A lifestyle hatched from an egg
Hong Kong consensus

Shek O in May

I always enjoyed loping down off the dragon.
An eastern electric rumble warned me one day
To leave the ridge and its conductive risks
So, I landed in Shek O, that peninsular enigma,
Where a clean swell marched through
And satyr-waves broke insatiably upon the bay

Rain was near, day-trippers were few
The village was in its downtime shift
Quiet, fragrant, settled and unusually visible
With a hearty whiff of hopeful thrift
Holding a palpable resignation for what is
And what will probably come

But,
Shek O seems appended to mansions of wealth
Where little is seen and less can be shown
In stately gardens, set deeply apart
With shaded stories and shadowy pasts
The bohemian beach a clever device
To ensure only sanctioned legends are known

Then as I strolled by in the varying light
A separate world was briefly revealed
And half-seen behind a glimpse-hedge of cane
Were fresh-fallen bauhinia leaves being swept
Lawns and customs close-clipped and well-kept
And fine grass still watered in a rich time of rain

Tai Tam

Tai Tam evokes mixed memories
Wartime resistance, occupation
Water security, exquisite scenes
Reminiscences invaded by sentiment
To permutate the difference
Between what is heard and what is felt
And refolded into a new history
By the origami of expedience

When walking the woods alone,
A choir of bulbuls claimed the canopy above me
With the bell-peal cadence of an avian anthem
In slightly shifting repeated phrases
From unselfconscious instinctive choices
To make an architecture of sunbird variations
That arrested and dissolved near-time
In the yearning reach of their ancestor's voices

So, in my memory, on that day
Tai Tam became a dais of saurian sound
Trees, birdsong, wind and water
Where deep-time connections can be found
And a further purpose can be glimpsed
In the lasting heart of the forest's song
By those who wish to see and feel
The natural future of Hong Kong

The choir in the canopy

Steep hillside forest
Treading softly, listening
The choir assembles

Tentative solo
Lifts the walker's reverie
Passerine-perfect

The full peal begins
Cadence from the canopy
Avian choral

Musical freedom
A gift to the listener
On this day alone

Birdcage

The aviary in Central is huge
And its birds are kept,
　　　　with great consideration
It is a luxurious cage,
　　　　without question
A perfect subtropical world,
　　　　behind wire
Encouraging avian breeding,
　　　　and industry
To produce nests, eggs,
　　　　and continuity
Eschewing conflicts and dispute
　　　　An aviary with a roof so high
Any instinct to escape,
　　　　is obviated
So, the free birds outside,
　　　　seem pitied or unseen
It tempts metaphorical comparison
　　　　and sits harmoniously in Hong Kong

The cooling ground

The living land feels restless once again
And deeper rumbles drown the wind and rain
So, Iceland shakes anew as Surtr stirs
Sending fire to forge the nascent plain

When Muspell and Niflheim mix their wares
Of heat and wet in mythic equal shares
To raise the mighty Ymir from its bed
And all its jotn-progeny from their lairs

Then, an innocent moment is truly found
As new stone springs glowing from the ground
A mesmeric bait in ripe-cherry red
Rim-stones forming with crunching-rock sound

This elvish perfection will not last long
When people start to sing the metal-song
And scour for lucre in the cooling rock
Dragging half-formed crystals from where they belong

What can shield the Earth from reckless plunder?
Is it human destiny to lay all asunder?
Will Thor be seduced by corporate greed?
Or will there be protection from the god of thunder?

In exuberance

Through a smoky morning mist
Fountains Abbey is looming grey
Its naked blockwork clear to see
The gritstones of a monkish life
Letting silent plainsong free

The sunrise lights the thinning fog
So now a blackbird in full voice
Provides a censer-sound of joy
Through the chancel and the choir
A gift to every girl and boy
To skip them to a higher plane
With soli deo set aside
To see all nature in the round
And in exuberance to abide

Cloister

Devoid of numinous and pomp
The cloister lends a cooling calm
Its shape a simple symmetry
That lifts distraction from its form
A place to pray and meditate
A living-space for vows upheld
With thought and time to dedicate
A life to higher aspiration

Some new cracks have now appeared
In several of the gothic arches
The work of weight and entropy
Is pulling on these subtle porches
They soon will need a mason's touch
As was the case since first foundations
Smoothly to mend the sanctum-stones
Free of specious complications

Meanwhile, a timid stock dove rests
Beneath the cloister's massive yew
A life-preserving brief respite
Sheltered from the falcon's view
The time will come when it must fly
And submit to Nature's ordained fate
That plunges from the spire above
The hawking-force of evolution

Blarney

Proclaimed holy stone
Drainer of all sound reason
Just click on the link

The Cloch na Blarnan
A lingam for a banshee
Kissed for your peril

Stone of destiny
Foundations of the feudal
Scone Abbey ruined

St Stephen's stone cross
Lightning-struck by Taranis
Commanded by Wren

Whetstone is ready
To strop the naïve weapon
Cold superstition

Sarcophagus

In a bitter winter wind
A great stone box exudes an aeolian moan
Standing in the corner of a stately garden
A lonely lawn-bound ornament
Trophy-spoil, foraged from a sandy grave
Stolen, emptied, displaced and displayed
Its tenant evicted; its hieroglyphs ignored
No due process, true permission or remorse
Gracing the ha-ha at the edge of the sward
As for the craftsmen who fashioned the piece
And those who commissioned the burial-safe
Such desecration they would count as a crime
Though they will never be known and never be asked
Their feelings erased by the passage of time
Remotely emotive from deep in the past
With no one of power to speak up at last
The sarcophagus will still hum its lament
While we search our hearts for strength to repent

Lighted

An ageing man breathed morning air
With mistle and robin, thrushly singing
Their coinciding spring duets
A blend of serendipity and sound
That soothed him on his daily round
Of weary streams and worry-meadows

He loved the lifting songbird notes
And sought to bring them to his heart
To still his agitated mood
Such music surely must prevent
The everlasting vague lament
That was his new companion

Then, as the days of spring grew long
A hopeful dawn infused his mind
And brought a lighted understanding
That there was no sense in mortal fear
As the crossing-over time draws near
To where the blackbirds sing forever

Shaping legends

A smoky wick-lit limestone cave
A haven for ten thousand years
Imprinted with collective life
And resonant with joys and fears
Made safe by sure possession

A place for stories in the warm
To learn the said-facts of the clan
Forebears' deliverances from harm
And how the family first began
Made true by repetition

With rapt attention to the tale
Small children listen to the chant
They hear the matriarch regale
Of wolf and bear and oliphant
Made light by long tradition

Sheltering in a rocky shell
Sitting around a hearth of stones
Is how we were and how we are
Shaping legends is in our bones
But now is,
Made brief by soft conditions

La Roche aux Fées

Ten of us travelled en famille
To picnic at La Roche aux Fées
Pulled by a magnetic force of time
To share a place with long-gone souls
Memorialized by the dolmen-mass
That hugely stands in stilling mood
Benignly granting leave to stay
To chatter-light and savour food
On a warm and glittering bee-bright day

Later we walked the gallery grave
With quietly reverent ritual-hush
Feeling the historic calming cool
Of the neolithic hand-made cave
There was no sense of morbid trespass
Projected by the looming stones
Nor any cryptic accusation
Of treading on deeper sacred bones
Just a welcome to the shadow-space

Curious moment

Mesozoic gems
Newly hewn and cast aside
Fossil detritus

Rarer is better
Contempt for common creatures
Ammonites ignored

Bigger is better
On Jurassic trophy hunts
Disney-fictive world

Curious moment
I lift a tossed rock and see
A perfect live snake

Possibilities

A mind in the making,
    growth
The way out, to find a frame
    that fits
Seeking the way, knowing the way
Through electric fields too small
    to know or measure
What tugs a raven's iron heart?
    all the possibilities
In the mysterious quantum tunnels
    of inspiration
Allowing the intuition of discovery,
    rule-curving inventions
Subverting complacent conventions
Mustering the confident art
    of the unsure
Ideas in the wake of a quark,
    and at its mercy
Naming the smallest worlds
Where all is not zero or one
    but a greyscale of everything
Such is the random shift of genes,
    that well of uniqueness
And such a lifeforce gift

Dry spell

To see a droughted river rising
Brings relief from coded worry
Languid fish have started darting
A flash of scales in the stormy sun
Welcome thunder-voice gives warning
Of falling ice and cleansing rain
Then to hear Reed Buntings calling
Adds a joy in the lowering light

Why do we feel so intensely
The brinkmanship of a long dry spell?
To celebrate with songs and dancing
As grasses sprout and rivers swell
It must be in our hard-wired nature
To seek the stream and artesian well
Legacy genes of the dry savannah
From Africa, whence we all hail

Gem-hoard

In the distant past
A stone-stealing myth-raven
Found a diamond

It stole many more
Hid them on a rocky ledge
Collecting began

Much time was wasted
Guarding the inedible
Preciousness defined

Many years later
The sacrificial gem-hoard
Was declared holy

The crow was lauded
For return on investment
Banking inducted

Brink

An umbrous man in greyscale hue
Plodded skyward with intent
The cliffs of Golden Cap to view
A rim-track skimmed along the drop
Leaning to its edging blocks
That framed that fascinating void
Where optic pulls come from the fog
And thin and piping siren-sounds
Advocate the quickest way

He stood before the solving deep
Until a wren's sharp saving-song
Kindled a gorsy beauty-flame
That ceased the sequence of his thoughts
So, the lonely walker reflected new
Upon the purpose of the place
He chose upon that autumn day
To match the growing darkness
Stony-etched into his face

The brink conveyed a pensive gift
Of time to think beyond the call
And take the longer harder path
Entering with grace the shadow-mist
To defy the demon's crow-black wrath
And rise up when the light returns
Because, this was not the time to fall

Out of the indigo

Catastrophe,
Throws a star chamber of defences
Around that egg of detachment
Where function rules
And notes of hope are flattened by a doubting smile
So even the songs of blackbirds lose their joy
Letting the creatures of superstition scratch the lid
Of a treasured box of logic, from within.
During the hectic tinnitus of near-sleep
With its cognitive twilight and synthetic demons
A cavernous encyclopaedia of possibilities
Drawn from the unlocked safe of half-sleep
That haunt the night and leave a stain on waking
But meet their subtle purpose of rehearsal
For a future of grief or restoration
So, we wait,
While natural ways are taken
Then slowly, we emerge,
Out of the indigo and into the light

Republic

Think of influence
And the power-strings of time
Repeating patterns

See then, the courtier
Keener than a forest jay
When the acorns fall

Hurry to bury
With no need for memory
Not seen, so not judged

The seeds lie hidden
Found at night by rats and pigs
Feral disposal

A few germinate
And grow to shape the future
Oaks of the daylight

Polishing stone

Stuck to the Earth in the Valley of Stones
Was found a witness to ancestral life
First claimed by people who came to this place
Seeking perfection from runcible rock
They lavished it with abraded attention
To form a subtle indelible trace

Grinding an axe on the polishing stone
With brittle trust and an uncertain fate
Common purpose, the best of their themes
Sharing the flint-craft's sharp finishing touch
Or plotting a land of conflicts and schemes
Through fine-edged weapons that splinter the bone

Or, shaping a hoe on the polishing stone
Perfecting the blade with consummate skill
While speaking of life and the hard sarsen sand
With fireside companions kept close at hand
Sharing a time of co-operative ease
By reverent hearths with fine tools to hone

And there it stands now, the polishing stone
An altar of options for five thousand years
Neutral techniques from which choices are made
Equally useful for adzes or spears
Witness to people who polished their plans
Of talking and fighting to settle the land

Working from home

At last!
The captive must be up and out
Running on a water-rising day
The clouds are higher, the gritstone drier
The brook is flushed near the parallel path
Carrying the smell and colour of peat
And making a clean cathartic sound
As background to the wren's bright song
The clearest call of all free souls
To stir a heart in the drifting mist

So, climbing in the dampened sun
The runner feels a weathered joy
Loping low though the heathered scrub
As a lapwing's pipe and a grouse's cackle
Are heard beyond a drystone wall
Just barely glimpsed in lichen-green
Marking the meaning of release
As aspirations stir and form
Across the hilltops after rain

Napping

An ageing hiker treads the rock
Along the track to Watendlath
And in the warm and weary breeze
Elects to rest beside the path

He leans back on a mossy scoop
Laughs at its sarcophagic fit
Between two massive granite slabs
Glacial dolmens framing it

The crickets in the bone-dry grass
Singing their soporific song
Loosen the leash of napping sleep
Then bring a midday dream along

He dreams of doors that start to close
And birds that can no longer fly
Of water that can flow uphill
Leaving the valleys grey and dry

Then,
On waking he is jaunty-fresh
Tramping the hills is such a joy
Tea and cake at the café next
Seventy years and still a boy

www.ingramcontent.com/pod-product-compliance
Lightning Source LLC
LaVergne TN
LVHW010306070426

835508LV00034B/3500

Viola, the Virgin Queen

None shall wear any velvet in gowns, furs of leopards, embroidery of silk: except the degrees and persons above mentioned, the wives of barons' sons, or of knights.

Cowls, sleeves, partlets, and linings, trimmed with spangles or pearls of gold, silver, or pearl; cowls of gold or silver, or of silk mixed with gold or silver: except the degrees and persons above mentioned; and trimmed with pearl, none under the degree of baroness or like degrees.

Enforcing Statutes of Apparel, issued at Greenwich, 15 June 1574, Elizabeth I

19

conceal me divulge nothing
I am a guiser and you are a
guiser revels mummers
memory and you

you whim
sical

Ruth Stacey

virgo not legs and thighs
of the bull fields
glean the corn attract
boy dressed as girl guised
as a boy arouses lord
erotic same
girl dressed as boy
courts lady erotic same
siblings slip swap exchange
son beams shines days

Ruth Stacey

Olivia as queen has a jester
fool take away the fool

amuse the queen jester
brother soul in heaven
so mourn no more fool
none shall wear any
carnation velvet
cloth of golde tissue
except duchess countess
all degrees above mentioned

Ruth Stacey

Viola, the Virgin Queen

'I send you, by the bearer a buck killed late last night by my hand, hoping, when you eat of it, you will think of the hunter...'

Henry VIII, *private letter to Anne Boleyn*

Ruth Stacey

beneath clothes weak and feeble
monthly bleeding tender
breasts saten damaske taffeta
above risen loaf throne diadem
locket ring conceals a mother
token circlet marriage no other
two Eliza V virgin Viola
both born in an hour
twin queen and girl disguised
prince salt water womb
neck cut death childbirth

Viola, the Virgin Queen

Viola, the Virgin Queen

Viola's father's house is white and red
her pious sister sickly brother dead
father knot impossible to untie
he had a mole upon his brow
she is all the children of his line
house corridors empty only screams
monument seat grief waiting
skin made of cloth mate reveal
to be a son one you must not
damaske elaborate figures
coat filled with four arms
blazon embolden lists
costly cloth masked covered
disguise is wickedness waxen frail

Ruth Stacey

green melancholy
grenian to flourish
long sleeves elegant
style inconstant lady
love sable yellow gold
gloomy geoluwian
fields cropped
frogs hazel eyes
blue grey shine
around the tower
thunder roars

Viola, the Virgin Queen

one hind my dear hunted chased
killed slim doe green velvet
bells sewn into the fabric musical
one to grow swell
truth no mistress no woman
you are all the brothers
of your father's house
lack of a man sun
unveiling blinded blazing

Ruth Stacey

imitate ornament
ruff layered robed image
create fakery brother
sickly youth not
brother of myself twin
myself male exact me

Viola, the Virgin Queen

her forehead yvory white
his instep warm and pale like just baked cake
her cheekes lyke apples which the sun hath rudded
his thighs weighted trunks in an unexpected storm
her lips lyke cherryes charming men to byte
his shoulders horizon like grassed tumps of earth
her brest lyke to a bowle of creame uncrudded
his cock lax as the skin of a fawn in long pasture
her paps lyke lyllies budded
his freckles like spilt tea leaves and dried petals
her snowie necke lyke to a marble towre
his disinterest in poetry sustains its creation

do not embrace me until I am Viola
when I have cast this male garb to the floor
and as I will never do that then embrace me
you prefer boys
never whisper never bees never
maiden weeds wild flowers wilt
blazon sun brother twin sister died
sit monument monstrous venom fountains
garments costume clothes damaske cloth cheek
I am all the brothers monstrous regiment bees

Ruth Stacey

Viola, the Virgin Queen

I am all the sisters of my father's house and all

the sons too

and yet I know
knot tied
unravelling
moðorslaga

six different
seek destruction spoil souls
more languages all your foibles
silver tissue white velvet
the slaughtered hind
owned cunning black eyes
I have them
mater moeder madre
mère μητέρα mam

NOTES

Lines used from:

'Epithalamion', by Edmund Spenser

Twelfth Night, by Shakespeare

'Letter to Anne Boleyn', by Henry VIII

The First Blast of the Trumpet, by John Knox

Enforcing Statutes of Apparel, issued at Greenwich, 15 June 1574, Elizabeth I

Glossary

Moðorslaga: Old English, matricide, mother-slayer

Mater, moeder, madre, mère, μητέρα, mam: Six different words for mother

DEDICATION

This pamphlet is dedicated to Prof Nicoleta Cinpoes for sowing the first seeds of this collection when I researched and pitched a PhD project idea about *Twelfth Night*, Elizabeth I, and the brother she should have been. Thank you for our inspiring and supportive conversations about the poems as I was drafting them.

Thanks, and gratitude to my collaborator Desdemona McCannon. It was a rosy-golden dream to have you illustrate my poems. @desdemonab

www.ingramcontent.com/pod-product-compliance
Lightning Source LLC
LaVergne TN
LVHW010305070426
835508LV00026B/3439